Mind-Blowing Client Experiences Can Be
Your Biggest Competitive Advantage

Written by Tammy Fink

ISBN: 9798702557519

Author: Tammy Fink

Cover Design: Tammy Fink

Printed in the United States of America

First Edition 2021

I dedicate this book to you, because I created this book for YOU. Everything that has gone into creating it was done to inspire, motivate, and celebrate with you.

You have my PERMISSION and ENCOURAGEMENT to write all over this book. Document your hopes and dreams for connecting with your clients. I want you to be able to refer back to this book each time you overcome a hurdle and achieve each milestone.

You've Got The Magic Within You,
& I Know You Love Your Clients...

Now, Let's Blow Their Minds With
Your WOW!Factor Experience!

XXXOOO

Tammy Fink
Chief WOW!Creator

Contents

:: CHAPTER ONE ::

GETTING STARTED: WOW!FACTOR EXPERIENCE

You may be asking yourself "What is a WOW!Factor Experience? More specifically how do I get one? And what will it cost?" Now, let's slow our roll here, this book is going to help answer all of your questions, and probably a few more that you didn't even know you had before this very moment.

So grab your beverage of choice, and let's start at the beginning. Introductions are probably in order, so this is as good a place to start as any. My name is Tammy Fink, and I have been a graphic designer and worked in marketing for over 30 years now, creating amazing logos and branding guides for hundreds of businesses. The one thing that I began noticing is that businesses typically fall into one of two categories. Either you are a virtual online entrepreneur or you are the brick and mortar variety with some sort of an online presence.

Whichever category you fit into, you're probably overwhelmed by running your own business and trying everything you can think of to 'stand out' from your competitors. When did it become ALL about the competition? So now instead of building your business, you are focusing on WINNING... you tell yourself after all, you must WIN because it's a competition.

Let's slow down for just a moment, and let's ask a couple of questions: "What would it look like if we didn't have to worry about the competition? What if you could create something so unique that you wouldn't need to worry about 'who else is doing what?" People would automatically flock to you and your brand because of something that YOU offered that NO ONE ELSE could, at least not in the same unique way as only you can. That my friend is why you need to create a WOW!Factor Experience for your clients.

Believe me when I say, a unique WOW!Factor Experience will blow your clients minds. And that will help you to not only keep more of your existing clients, but also attract new ones.

▶ Get out of the box.

In the fall of 2015, amidst trending social memes of seasonally delicious "pumpkin-spice-mocha-latte-cappuccino-isms", I began looking to create my own WOW!Factor Experience. I began wondering, "What could I offer my clients that wasn't being offered by everyone else in my space"?

I thought about creating more memberships and courses, after all I had created a couple of courses over the years: **How To Plan Your Own Planner For Your Tribe** and the now infamous **Legendary Logo Bootcamp.** But everyone these days has a course, or a webinar, or a workshop. Everyone wanted to be different and offer something unique to their clients or tribe. So, what if it's not our offering or product that makes us stand out?

Every month, entrepreneurs are scrambling to 'fill' their programs with new people. The focus is almost entirely on the 'numbers'. Why isn't anyone focusing on the people meaning the clients that you already have. Could we increase client retention, and get more clients at the same time? What could we offer that allows us to do more than just create raving fans? So I began developing what would become my Client-centric Connection framework.

"I mean after all, it feels pretty amazing to have your very own tribe. And while most marketing plans will show you how to get clients, what they don't show you is how to keep them. No one wants to watch their tribe disappear every month. Most clients leave a program because they feel disconnected. Oh, sure you could just get new clients every month. But, what if I could show you how to create added value, and keep your tribe happier and more engaged. Strategic touch-points could increase your client retention up to 30% or higher. Anchor your tribe with Meaningful & Memorable touch-points that will allow your tribe to really connect with you."

– Tammy Fink

Traditional marketing has you focus on features and benefits of your product. And while this is very effective, it's not what ultimately helps you to stand out in the market. I want you to not only 'THINK outside the box'. I want you to get out of the box completely, well at least for now. With the WOW!Factor Experience it is crucial that you understand that it isn't just about how YOU are different from your competition, it is how you *CONNECT WITH YOUR CLIENTS DIFFERENTLY* that makes you stand out. No one else can do it exactly the way you do, because you and the people you connect with are unique.

When you offer your clients strategic touch-points to interact with you and your business, you are encouraging and developing a stronger client relationship with them from the start. It's truly a unique client experience that they won't get from anyone else. I will explain how to put the focus on the client and increase your client retention at the same time through building a Client-centric Connection.

You'll learn what your clients are truly wanting from you and your program, and not just what you are providing for them. You will create more WOW!s, increase more sales, extend the lifetime value of your customers, and elevate your products and services in the marketplace.

▶ Creating a Client-centric Connection.

A Client-centric Connection is more than just converting prospects into clients, or building a community of raving fans, it's about true connection and client retention. It's about paving a way for your audience, partners, and clients to not only buy from you over and over again, but to also refer you to their friends and champion your mission. It's about motivating, celebrating, and inspiring your clients in a way that only you can do.

Traveling through the Client-centric Connection framework, you will understand how you can begin to connect with your tribe on a whole other level and create a client retention plan that could last a lifetime. You want to make an impact on the world. And who doesn't want hand hearts from their tribe? The most effective Client-centric Connection opportunity falls somewhere between "thank-you for your purchase" and "let's get married". And since we aren't trying to freak out your clients on the first date, let's see how you can make this happen. So carry on, hand-heart makers. We could all use more hand-hearts in our lives.

▶ Knowing the Whos in my Who-ville

At this stage of the game, you probably know who it is that you are serving. But before we get started there are some things that you need to know about those people...

...who are the "Whos" that make up your "Who-ville" really?

These could be the people that you serve, your team, your vendors perhaps, and the referrals that they all give you. And don't forget the people who help you get your message out there such as, podcasters, influencers, affiliates, and guests. Include all of your people: clients, members, affiliates, vendors, everyone. Make a list of these people and what roles they play in your business. Who are they?

And once you identify them, do this one very important thing...take care of them. These are your 'Whos": all of the people, in your tribe, your inner-circle, and your team. You need to get connected with them for them to feel that they are important to you, and your program. And stay connected throughout your client's journey.

Before you can connect in a way that is truly meaningful to your 'Whos', you need to know a few more pieces of information. After all it's not about you, it's about them. Let's get started. So who are the 'Whos' in your 'Who-ville?' On the next page, make a list of at least 25 of people you want to connect with and build a stronger relationship. If you don't have a full list people that you know, add in people with whom you would like to connect. Don't worry what this will cost, or how you will connect at this point.

Start here:

1. ______________________________

2. ______________________________

3. ______________________________

4. ______________________________

5. ______________________________

6. ______________________________

7. ______________________________

8. ______________________________

9. ______________________________

10. ______________________________

11. ______________________________

12. ______________________________

13. ______________________________

14. ______________________________

15. ______________________________

16. ______________________________

17. ______________________________

18. ______________________________

19. ______________________________

20. ______________________________

21. ______________________________

22. ______________________________

23. ______________________________

24. ______________________________

25. ______________________________

▶ What makes my clients tick?

Do you know your demographics and psycho-graphics of your clients? In other words, what makes them 'tick' and where they are doing their 'ticking'. Most entrepreneurs may know their clients demographics, but that doesn't give you the big picture about your clients at all — humans are complicated, to say the least.

To build a relationship with your clients, you need to develop and express empathy for them. Walk a mile in their shoes during every interaction and step of your program, product, or service, and then take the relationship a step further. Get to know your clients.

- What has brought them to this moment in time?
- What keeps them awake at night?
- What frustrations and joys do they feel?
- What is their story, and why do you care about them?
- What do they love and what do they hate?
- Do they drink coffee or tea?

Make it a habit for you and your team to jot down notes either on paper, or in a CRM (Customer Relationship Management) system. Oh yes, that is totally a thing, and you probably already have one. So use it to make some WOW! notes about your clients.

Understanding this and more will ensure that your content will connect with them on a whole other level. And you will be able to offer them connection points unlike anyone else. It will truly be a unique client experience. (I will talk about this in a later chapter.)

▶ Isn't it a numbers game?

Getting clients and keeping them are two entirely different things when it comes to business. Your initial business goal is obviously acquiring new clients. But discovering how you can retain these clients and their revenue can increase your profits anywhere from 25% to 95%. Why is that?

Research has shown that clients tend to buy more from a company that they have already done business with over doing business with someone else that they don't know, like, or trust. While business is always a numbers game, that doesn't mean that you aren't required to invest some of those 'numbers' back into your people through time and money. You need to create a line item in your overall budget for relationship-building. If you are a numbers person, then I'm sure you are asking yourself right now, "What kind of investments are we talking about here? "

Plan on 'pouring-back' into your clients 5-10% of THEIR investment in YOU. If your program costs $500 then spend at least $50 on your client. If your program is $20,000 over a years time... then spend $1,000-2,000 on them over the next year. Same with your time investment. If your program lasts a year, plan on spending a minimum of 18 days during that year in connection with your clients (live or virtual). This could be 1:1 conversations, retreats, gifts, or notes. Anything that will inspire, celebrate, or motivate your client along their journey with you. This is going to increase your client retention, among a great many other benefits to you and your business. And it will also make for a more amazing experience for your clients.

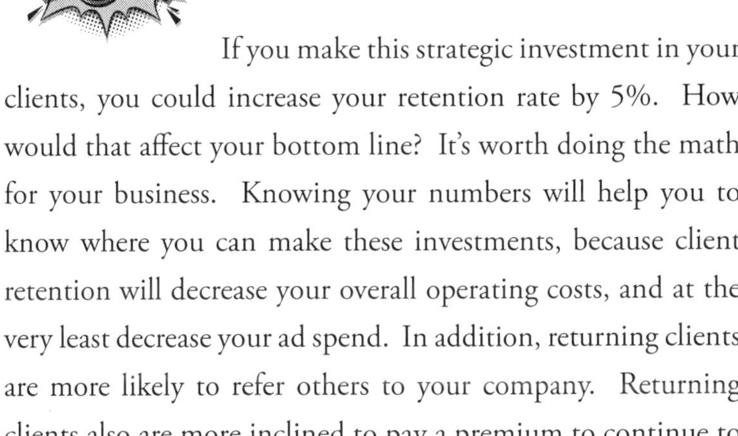

If you make this strategic investment in your clients, you could increase your retention rate by 5%. How would that affect your bottom line? It's worth doing the math for your business. Knowing your numbers will help you to know where you can make these investments, because client retention will decrease your overall operating costs, and at the very least decrease your ad spend. In addition, returning clients are more likely to refer others to your company. Returning clients also are more inclined to pay a premium to continue to do business with you, rather than going somewhere else and starting over. So, a 5% increase means a lot to you and your business.

Are you beginning to understand the idea of client connection and are envisioning what that connection could mean for your business? When people start talking about sales, whether it's in the virtual space or the brick and mortar world, people think that it's only a numbers game.

Numbers are important for sure when you are running a business. But it's not the most important thing. When you get a client, your focus should be on them first.

- What does your client need and want from you?
- When can you celebrate, motivate, or inspire them?
- How can you establish a relationship with them that will last?
- How can you make it easy for them to share their experience with others?

▶ Why are my clients doing business with me?

I have had clients that have worked with me from the beginning of my company. And some clients who have changed jobs, and took me with them when they went to the next company. So, not only did I keep the company they had been working with, but gained a new one in the process. My success has been built on developing relationships, within the amazing service I was providing. It wasn't one without the other. My clients could have gone anywhere to get a logo designed, or packaging created. But it was ME who they wanted to work with, I gave them a unique client experience that they couldn't get anywhere else. And this became my secret sauce, my very first WOW!Factor Experience. My clients felt valued and heard. So, I focused on how I could better serve my clients, and put them first. It became about them.

And more than that, I wanted to create relationships with the vendors who helped me to create the products for my clients and their clients, and when they referred me to their peers. It's a ripple effect, like throwing a small pebble in a pond. Your business affects everyone, and it's more than just simply a product or service.

Do you know why your clients are doing business with you? I have taken courses online, been a part of memberships and masterminds many times over the years. And I find it amazing that sometimes the owners of those businesses are so disconnected from their tribes. I have seen it happen many times, where the business owner decides it's 'time' to change things, and they start hacking and shrinking their offers. Sometimes they 'cut' the very thing that had initially drawn their members to their program in the first place. So once you have a tribe, it's important to develop a clear understanding of why people are doing business with you.

▶ So, where do I start?

You start where everyone starts: At The Beginning. You 'know' your clients, but let's take a look at additional information that you should be gathering from them. For instance do you know your people's birthdays? Do you know their addresses? What about their email addresses? Now, you may think that these things seem 'basic' but the reasons that you need to know these things, (and more) is not basic in the least. It's critical data for relationship building. Here is an idea list that you can use to see what you could be and probably should be tracking.

1. Name

2. Shipping Address

3. Website

4. Email Address

5. Birthday

6. Social Media Preferences

7. Previous Purchases

8. Which Podcasters or Influencers do they follow?

9. Beverage of choice (coffee, tea, wine, beer, ?)

10. Favorite Restaurant

11. Marriage Status

12. Kids?

13. Pets?

14. Clothing sizes: T-Shirt Size/Sock Size/Shoe Size

15. Favorite Vacations

16. Personality

17. Who is on their team?

18. Do they travel for business?

19. What was the last training they attended?

20. Favorite Author

21. What trade organizations do they belong to?

22. ____

23. ____

24. ____

Now this is not an extensive list at all. Based on your particular product or service, try to think of ways that you can track information that will allow you to deliver a more customized experience with you and your company. Does your client work from home or do they have an office? Do they work independently or have a team? Perhaps you should consider how to WOW! them, and perhaps their family as well.

I love the story that John Ruhlin shares in his book "Giftology". This heart-centric tycoon of the corporate gifting world notes that within his own corporation he gifts his employees as well. John arranges for a cleaning service for his employees' private homes, and has their cars detailed on special holidays. The brilliant part of this is the experience for not only the employee, but it spills over to their family and friends too. This kind of connection builds loyal bonds. And if this works in the corporate world, why wouldn't it work in the virtual arena as well?

Well actually it does work in both worlds, and it's an amazing opportunity for you to be able to WOW! your clients from day one. When you establish strong relationships with everyone from your team to your clients by showing them love, the loyalty bond that is built will solidify the relationship. It's not just a temporary gift, it's something that keeps you in your client's mind all year long. Create lifelong, bucket list experiences for your clients, and they will remember you long after that initial sale.

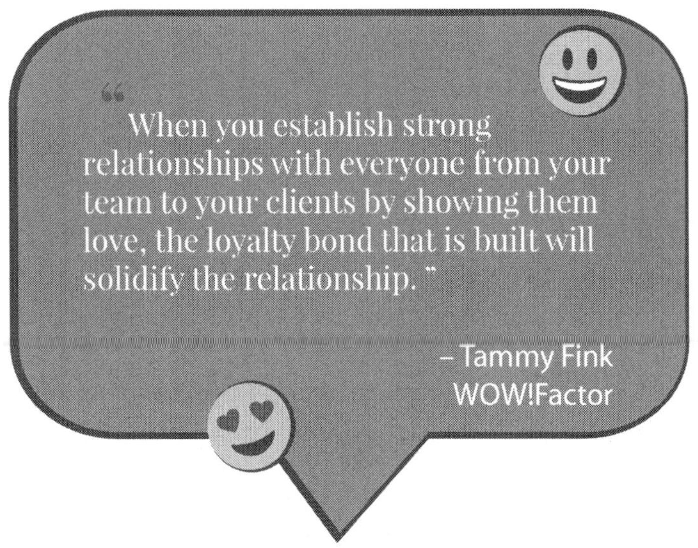

▶ How am I different?

There is just something about you that makes you stand out. Some might say that it's your "super-power." Imagine if you were to take your 'super-power,' whatever that might be for you, and add HOW your client engages with you. That then becomes your WOW!Factor Experience, which is the unique client experience that you offer.

In fact, your WOW!Factor Experience could be the biggest competitive advantage that you have. And it's the very thing that makes your clients want to 'hang out with you'...and throw credit-cards at you every time you offer a new product or service. Ask yourself:

- What matters to my clients?
- What makes them giddy with excitement?
- What is their love language for the process?
- What will they remember about working with me?

To determine what will be your WOW!Factor Experience, you must first explore your client journey, and the touch points that you will offer. Over the last decade, I have developed and championed this technique I call the Client-centric Connection Process which is the basis of your WOW!Factor Experience. The recipe for an amazing connection is to take one part hospitality, and add many touch-points for your clients, and mix well with your very own super-power.

There are five phases to building an amazing WOW!Factor Experience for your clients:

GREAT OPPORTUNITIES
TO WOW! YOUR CLIENTS...
HOSPITALITY
WELCOME
LAUNCHES
HIGH
FIVES
NEXT
STEPS
ONBOARDING
FIRST
DAYS
MILESTONES
THANK
YOU
AWARD-WINNING
PERFORMANCES
TEAM
BUILDING
TESTIMONIALS
LIFE
CELEBRATIONS
INSPIRED
EVENTS

1. Welcome Home

2. Connection Building

3. Unique Client Experience

4. Client Retention

5. Advocacy

We start here because they are the most impactful part of your client's journey. In each of these five you should look for ways to either Inspire, Motivate, or Celebrate your clients. This technique will help you to create your own unique client experience, and connect with your clients in a way that will surprise and delight them throughout their entire journey with you. Let's look at the these five phases, and then I will expand on them in the following chapters.

▶ Welcome Home

Focusing on making your clients feel special from the very beginning of your relationship. What can you do to welcome them in a way that feels very special, and is simple for you or your team to implement? Use personal information to develop touch points that help you to connect on a deeper level with your clients.

Establish an amazing on-boarding or welcome practice that celebrates your new clients and helps them to acclimate to your brand culture from the beginning. Increased profits, client accountability, referrals, and loyalty would be guaranteed from their very first touch-point with you and your business. It is totally worth the investment into your client's experiences.

▶ Client-centric Connections

Create more M&Ms… Meaningful and Memorable products that bridge the gap between virtual (online) and tangible (up close and personal). You are connecting with real human beings, so make heart to heart connections that will really matter. This will make a huge difference in your business, as it's not just a "nice to have". These Client-centric Connections will increase client retention, and build raving fans.

▶ Unique Client Experience

The client experience that you offer will differentiate you from your competition. No one can duplicate the experience you provide. Do you have ways for your clients to engage with you that is repeatable? The client experience can be a cornerstone to your business. Engaging with your clients is something you must do to build your business. But how well you do it is completely up to you. Delivering an amazing client experience should be your focus, but establishing client engagement is your marketing strategy to get there.

▶ Client Retention

Plan strategies for keeping your clients more engaged to achieve higher client retention. There is probably a voice screaming in your head right now that is saying "we must have more clients/customers". It isn't just about the numbers. In the rush to bring in new people, you could be overlooking those with whom you already have a relationship.

What about your community? Even in the online space, it costs more to acquire new members than it does to maintain your existing ones. Now, think about that for just a moment and ask yourself: What would happen if you focused more on client retention, and planned for it before even finding your next client?

▶ Advocacy

Give your clients an amazing way to tell others about you and your product or services. This is just good business sense. However, many entrepreneurs simply overlook this phase when they build their business. Shouldn't people just automatically know how to promote or give positive testimonials about great service? Well, perhaps they should.

Make it a habit of asking other people, "How can I tell others about you?" Or "What can I say in my 'review' that will help you the most"? And you will soon find out that many people just haven't given it any thought. If even YOU don't know how they can help you, how could your clients begin to give you testimonials that really help you to move the needle.

Creating advocacy and loyalty opportunities around your business will help you to gain more and more clients who want the same experience. It helps build better relationships through encouragement and support. And this support will help you to build a more impactful brand.

Take a moment and make a note of which of the five you would like to focus on over the next month: Welcome, Connection, Experience, Retention, and Advocacy.

:: CHAPTER TWO ::

WELCOME HOME { phase one }

New clients should have opportunities to learn about your product and community from day one. In the days of selling one-off products, especially in a corporate environment, the first sale is the goal. Done and done. However, with online products, up-sells, joint ventures, and affiliate opportunities, that initial sale is only the beginning of the relationship. It is so important to your bottom-line that you KEEP that client long after that first touch-point. You need to extend your client experience beyond that first sale.

In the online space, most everyone has some form of a digital product. But the often overlooked secret sauce is in creating hands on touch-points that could include a physical product or welcome box to help build client connection from the start. So how does your welcome process help you to retain your clients?

▶ How do I welcome clients?

You might be familiar with the term "on-boarding" when it comes to new employees, but what about your clients, or members? On-boarding is just a way of welcoming your clients to your program, membership, or training.

And Welcome Boxes have become a standard part of this on-boarding or welcome experience, and a great tangible way to start out the relationship with your clients. Think of your Welcome Box as more of a gift, than a swag opportunity. Putting the client's needs in front of your need for marketing your business will help you to create a life-long client, instead of a one-time customer.

I had a client whose on-boarding for her attendees signing up for her $3,500 signature program consisted of a hand-written note, and a small sticker of her logo for their laptop. While technically nothing she was doing up to this point could be considered 'wrong', it was definitely not earth shattering. In fact, I would say it barely registered a 'meh' on the WOW! Client Experience Meter.

WOW! CLIENT EXPERIENCE METER

We analyzed the overall intention of her program, and constructed a Welcome Box that would allow for her to provide a client-experience that was strategic, as well as impactful to her program. Her clients would be spending the next 30 days immersed in her life changing program. We looked at how we could best support them as they began this journey with her. Her Welcome Box is sure to be remembered and a shared experience throughout her entire program. The welcome is first step of what will be your whole WOW!Factor Experience created to continue to surprise and delight your clients throughout their journey. This initial touch-point gives them a look as to what they can continue to expect from doing business with you. And if done strategically, it's an amazing way to solidify the Client-centric Connection relationship.

As you can see, Welcome Boxes have become an excellent way to connect with people early on in the relationship, and encourage them to become loyal clients. Russell Brunson, online entrepreneur and creator of Click Funnels coined the term "funnel hacking". And his tribe members have embraced the nomenclature: Funnel Hackers. Russell has created an entire community where 'Funnel Hackers' are celebrated. Beginning with welcome boxes and "Funnel Hacker" t-shirts to milestone designations, such as the ultimate achievement of his program being the "Two Coma Club" for his millionaire Funnel Hacker members.

GREAT IDEAS FOR YOUR WELCOME BOXES

- ENCOURAGEMENT GIFTS
- MESSAGE BUTTONS
- GRATITUDE MESSAGES

- SOCIAL MEDIA SHARE-ABLES
- COMMUNITY LANGUAGE
- BOOKS OF INTEREST
- PREMIERE FUTURE EVENTS/PROGRAMS
- EXCLUSIVE ITEMS

You are probably going to need to write some things down:

GREAT IDEA: Include books that you have personally read and endorse the message of the author. Take a moment and list as many as you can below.

This is an excellent way to build a venture opportunity with other trainers, entrepreneurs, and authors. What if you are an author yourself, or have training materials that will help your clients to obtain success through your program? Of course, you should include those items in your program's welcome box. If you are an author, a custom journal or planner would make for an excellent companion piece that is only available in your welcome box. These types of materials encourage an exclusivity component that makes your offer truly irresistible.

____

____

____

____

____

____

____

____

____

____

JUST A BAD IDEA: "Something is better than nothing." This statement isn't always true. When you are picking items for your Welcome Boxes, stay away from using cheap carnival trinkets, or bite size candy. It's kind of like when you went trick or treating as a kid, sure you knew you would get the snack-size candy all over town. But there was always a line at the house that was giving away full size candy-bars. That was the place everyone wanted to be, and you didn't want to miss out on the experience.

Remember you are aiming for a WOW!Factor Experience. If you aim for 'we have to give them something' chances are that's how it will feel to your clients. Not exactly what we are going for here. You don't have to spend a ton of money, but your Welcome Box is probably going to be one of your client's first experiences with you and your program and they know how much they have spent with you up to this point. So make this touch-point worth their time and yours

What if you established an amazing on-boarding practice, that celebrated your new clients and helped them to acclimate into your membership culture from the beginning? What if you could create a welcome buzz within the social media world, that would guarantee that people would be referring to their friends, and other acquaintances, to your membership or community? The increase in profits, accountability, referrals, and loyalty, would be guaranteed from their very first touch-point with your company. What an amazing experience for everyone…right from the beginning.

So how do we do this exactly? Here are four key on-boarding practices to ensure an amazing on-boarding experience for your tribe or membership.

▶ Focus on client retention from the beginning.

Often, there is such a rush to bring in more new members while not really considering the existing members within a community site. It costs more to acquire new members than it does to maintain existing ones. Now, think about that for just a minute…what if you focused more on client retention, and did it before they were even your client. You wouldn't have to work nearly as hard or spend nearly as much money if you just focused on taking care of who you already have in your membership, or as a part of your client base. I have included a whole chapter on Customer Retention coming up.

▶ Oh, yeah & personal connection matters.

I am a huge fan of Andrew & Pete from *ATOMIC.* If you don't know them, well… you totally should check them out. They have an amazing and fun content marketing community-based in the UK with an extraordinary YouTube channel. And they have been featured on sites such as Inc., Huffington Post, Social Media Examiner, Convince and Convert, Entrepreneur on Fire and Kim Garst. These guys are practically famous. And since I have a secret plan to help them take over the world.... I had asked them to share with me a bit about their journey developing their on-boarding process for their community. And this is what they said...

"A couple of years into our membership, we looked at our retention rate, and decided that it needed to be higher. So we started looking at how we could completely revitalize the welcoming process. In just a short few months, we were able to double our retention rates and increase our referrals massively simply by improving the on-boarding process. It's not about a few welcome emails, it's about having contact and making them truly feel like they are a part of something. People come for the content, but stay for community, the friendships and connections they make. Personal connection matters, and if you can process/automate/delegate/scale that then you're onto a winner!

- Andrew & Pete

▶ **Making culture tangible.**

This ain't your mama's SWAG! The harsh reality is people

really don't want to wear your logo, they want to be a part of your mission, a part of your story! If your community or company culture resonates with your clients, then they want to be a part of something bigger than themselves, and they can be eager to spread the word. Remember the 'Funnel Hackers' example. How do you make your culture tangible?

First, you start by, establishing your company mantra. Now pay attention to how your clients interact with it. Do your clients react with hand-hearts or fist pumps? Do they have community names for referring to your tribe or members?

Next, get to know your culture. Know how you want your clients to feel every time they interact with you, your brand, your employees, your products, and your events. Is your culture oozing out every pore of your collective being? Your clients will come to expect this culture from you. And this isn't something you can fake. Over time, people will know if you are being genuine and authentic, or not. If you can deliver, and give them what they expect every time—you are golden. You don't have to spend a lot of money, but you do have to be consistent.

SOMETHING TO CONSIDER: Look at the details of your brand that will help you to create things that people will wear or own proudly to show that they are part of a tribe or community. Your mission should be front and center. And on-boarding is an amazing time to let your members know that they are a part of something special. Create something tangible to show that they matter, and are an appreciated part of the team. This encourages them to become part of the woven fabric of your membership or community's mission.

▶ The whole membership experience.

While it's true that your client journey begins at the on-boarding process, and no doubt that it's very important to start off with your best foot forward. Determining where you want to take your client next should be a big part of the on-boarding sequence as well. It's equally as important to start building good habits from the onset.

The on-boarding sequence can help your clients navigate through your processes and procedures. Encouraging them to be accountable and become an integral part of your community. This personal connection helps you to create an investment for the life of your members. If your on-boarding is done right, your clients are now fully involved in your process. And FOMO takes over, oh, yeah…it's a real thing.

More notes? Okay you got it...

WOW!Factor

:: CHAPTER THREE ::

CLIENT-CENTRIC CONNECTION { PHASE TWO }

How do you connect with your clients? Quite simply... put your clients first. Listen to what THEY want...they will help you make some of the most important decisions about your business, including how to connect with them. Clients who are engaged with your brand will stay with your brand. This is what is meant by a Client-centric Connection.

▶ Focus on your clients first.

Some of the most successful corporate businesses start with a Client-centric Connection perspective. Truett Cathy, the owner of **Chick-fil-A** always said that he was NEVER in the chicken business. He was in the people business. Howard Schultz, the founder of Starbucks, built an entire business where coffee is the product, but the customer service and overall experience is the top priority. Even Disney is renowned for their customer experience, and moments of amazement for even their youngest customer.

Where are your opportunities for WOW!Factor Experiences within your business? Once you determine the touch-points throughout your customer journey, then you will discover your WOW!Factor Experience moments for each of those opportunities. And you should strive to get really good at finding these moments. Simply put, WOW!Factor Experience moments are your opportunity to create "WOW!" responses from your team, customers, clients, or community.

I had been in the graphic design industry for over 30 years. I have created hundreds and hundreds of logos, and worked with amazing global brands. I've designed many brochures, business cards, billboards and almost anything you can imagine, and I still do. But, while the companies' brands were amazing, and they had some sweet swag, I noticed that they were still experiencing lots of client churn, and they were constantly stressed trying to keep up with their competition. And that's when I discovered that Client-centric Connections make all the difference. And I started working with my customers to create products that allowed them to not only stand out from their competition, but to give their clients something that only they could deliver…a unique client experience. This leads to more WOW!s from their clients and more hand-hearts for them.

▶ M&Ms make all the difference.

The secret RECIPE to amazing WOW!s…everything must be measured by M&Ms. No, not the chocolate M&Ms. I believe that all connections should have two criteria and it doesn't matter if the connections were virtual or in real life. Wow! Experience moments should always be measured by being both Meaningful and Memorable {M&Ms} to the client.

These WOW!Factor Experience moments can bring your clients to tears, it's something that you can deliver that makes your client's feel seen and heard. Simply put, it's a gift or an acknowledgment of an event that impacts their lives. And it shows that you remembered something they said that mattered to them. Your clients want to know that they are appreciated and celebrated.

▶ Creating WOW!s for my clients.

Build good habits from the beginning. This helps everyone to clearly see the next step, and know where the client journey is taking them. I love using physical products like journals and planners to help communicate the client journey and your program to your members.

Planners are an excellent way to build accountability into a daily plan that keeps your clients, members, or fans eyeballs on your mission every single day. While digital products can be the latest and greatest technology available, if your client base is less than professional IT developers, it might be more strategic to keep it low tech and accessible to everyone. Not to say that you can't have PDF versions of your physical products. That can be a win as well.

These types of physical products can be a part of your on-boarding procedure. Why not include them in a custom Welcome box? Or a Congratulations You Have Achieved The Next Phase box? Create these WOW!s for your people and they will tell everyone they know, especially on social media. Just ask them to share photos of their welcome boxes with family and friends. This is your program, your system, your products, and your members take good care of them.

With strategic execution, they will be around to take care of you in the long run.

The WOW!s that I have experienced, been involved with, or have helped other entrepreneurs create have ranged from little things like Hot Wheels cars that give a touch-point to a key note speech, to t-shirts for introverts to wear to social events that start conversations for them. Again it's really about building connections with your tribe or membership. Some people do it very well...and it makes a difference in the whole client experience. While these moments are planned and strategic, all great WOW!s feel extremely custom and special to those involved.

Again, look at it from the perspective of your client first, this encourages the Client-centric Connection. What would they want from you? What are the first things they need to know? And how can you make that learning experience an EVENT? Give them their very own WOW!s.

▶ Amazing client experiences build connections.

We know that it takes a lot of effort for entrepreneurs to stand out against the competition. With so many websites, social media groups, free downloads, email blasts, videos, and informative webinar offerings, differentiating yourself to prospective clients can be a difficult and large undertaking. Creating a unique client experience assures that you offer something that others just can't compete with. You will stand out with your client-appreciation and experiences.

While active social media content and email campaigns can keep your digital clients engaged for the moment. It doesn't necessarily mean that your clients feel appreciated and connected with you enough to stick around for the long term. An in-person or virtual event is an excellent WOW!Factor Experience touch-point opportunity and a way for you to connect with your clients. You can also use the event to express gratitude, build personal engagement and make clients so happy they tell their friends and family about you. A successful client-experience event can give you the chance to make a huge difference in your client's life, create more raving fans, which leads to even more referrals.

Your clients are REAL people no matter which space they

are in. And focusing on Amazing Client Experiences...lets your clients know that they are important. Your experiences should be created within your company CULTURE. Here are some out-of-the-box event ideas sure to make your current clientele happy, and capture prospective clients:

- RETREATS
- ZOOM VIRTUAL MEETUPS
- CONCERTS
- EVENTS
- DINNERS
- AWARD RECOGNITION
- GAMES
- MUSIC
- SPIRITUAL/MEDITATION

- MASSAGE/SELF CARE
- FOOD TRUCK EVENTS
- ART PAINTING CLASSES
- POTTERY WORKSHOPS
- HOME OFFICE ORGANIZATION PARTIES
- ONLINE GAME SHOWS
- EXCLUSIVE TOURS
- CHEF DINNERS
- WORKSHOPS
- GRAND SELFIE OPPORTUNITIES
- TEAM BUILDING
- PHOTO SCAVENGER HUNTS

- HEART TO HEART CONVERSATIONS

- 1:1 LIVE CHATS

- TRAINING CRUISES

▶ My company feels like home.

Be friendly and generous within the hospitality of your company. Be helpful and encourage opportunities to rave about your clients and promote them to each other. And allow your clients to rave about you.

I'm a huge Chip & Joanna fan, I just can't help it. During an interview I saw online, they explained that they enjoy connecting with customers and fans of Magnolia Market in Waco. Through touch-points they have built an experience around allowing customers to share their experiences. I think this is crucial to establishing long term authenticity for a company.

According to one article, the Magnolia Market customer satisfaction scores reach well into the 90+ percentile. However, they strategically pick their moments when deciding to send a 'how did we do?' email survey after a customer shares a personal experience. They also encourage their customer service agents to 'connect' with their visitors through lunches, and they even have a budget for sending flowers or buy gift cards (not Magnolia ones) to give to customers.

At Magnolia Market, they have created an experience around allowing customers to share their own experiences with the world. This summer I spent some time 'vacationing' in Waco, so that I too could experience the world that Chip and Joanna built. It was amazing, and I really enjoyed the 'gamification' that was built into the experience as well, I will talk more about that in another chapter coming up. They have really leveled up the feeling of hospitality in their business.

How can you use hospitality when building your unique experiences for your clients?

WOW!Factor

:: CHAPTER FOUR ::

UNIQUE CLIENT EXPERIENCE { PHASE THREE }

What would happen if you stopped focusing on your competition? What if you started looking at your client's experience? When people talk about client experience, you hear a lot about BAD client experiences. When was the last time you had a BAD Customer Experience? I bet you have stories you can share about at least one of these brands. Do you have a brand that you LOVE?

▶ Customer loyalty from the start.

Let's take a look at an amazing example: How much do you love coffee? Coffee lovers take their love and commitment to their beverage of choice seriously. Some people have even written songs about it, gotten tattoos of it, or decorated their kitchens in homage to the bean juice. One of the best-loved coffee brands in the world is Starbucks… A friend of mine is a Starbucks junkie…

Globally, Starbucks has brilliant marketing…after all, they have convinced us that .50¢ worth of coffee has a street value of $8.00. But that's not my point. Let me tell you this story… As, I said I have a friend who LOVES Starbucks…looooves it. She eats there every day, not even kidding. So she had jumped on social media… "Rant-splaining" that while she loves Starbucks, she absolutely hates the Starbucks near her house. So, I had asked her:

"What is the deal with Starbucks down the street?" And she tells me…that they constantly get her order wrong. At first, she didn't quite understand why when she always ordered the same thing: Trenta Black Tea Lemonade with Super Light Ice and three Splenda, with no simple syrup and a double smoked bacon sandwich with no cheese…like 7 to 10 times in a month…they got it wrong.

She even complained to the manager, and they gave her a $20 Starbucks Gift Card. She gave them two more times, and they still messed up her order. She surmised that it must be just carelessness at this point. They just didn't care about the customer, and specifically they didn't care about her.

Now she could have converted to Duncan Donuts at this point…and who could have blamed her? She would have to change everything and would have had to explain to the Duncan's crew that by Trenta she meant the 31 oz. Big Gulp size coffee.

And she was probably just about to do it, when she discovers another Starbucks. This Starbucks is 30 minutes away from her house, but it has become her Most Favorite Starbucks.

Why is that Starbucks so great? It's not because it's convenient. It's not because they have more time to wait on clients. It's not even that they have a better product. Well, first of all…they know her by name. They know the majority of what she orders and when she orders it. They have started asking her if she will have her regular order. You remember the one: Trenta Black Tea Lemonade with Super Light Ice and three Splendu, with no simple syrup and a double smoked bacon sandwich with no cheese.

And in fact they are crazy busy there…all the time. She shared her latest adventure there…when she went in there were 6 people behind the counter working. The line is 10 people deep, but they still took the time to recognize her and call her by name. In fact, they were being friendly and attentive to each and every client. And at the same time, they were working on a phone in order of 30 coffees. All while maintaining amazing client service in the lobby, and drive-thru.

And she would have understood if they got HER order wrong, but they didn't. With everything going on, they still managed to get her order 100% right. She didn't want to change brands, but there was something that she wanted that her previous Starbucks didn't offer her.

So what did she want? I mean really? If the difference isn't even the product offering, what is it? The difference between the two different locations of the same store was the customer experience. She was demanding a BETTER CUSTOMER EXPERIENCE from her existing brand! The second Starbucks worked as a team and showed her that they care about their customers, all of their customers. And that made all the difference.

What would make an awesome client experience for your clients? Can you think of something that would be an amazing client experience? Something that is completely over the top, and unexpected. What if you could climb a mountain with your team? Or backpack across Europe with your coaching clients? Those experiences would be amazing. Do you have to go to this extreme to deliver an Amazing Customer Experience? The answer might surprise you, so just keep reading.

▶ Everything has already been done.

Maybe you are dreaming of offering something totally unique and unexpected... but then you start thinking that everything has already been done. Maybe you think competition has already done it all.

Or have they? Well, we will see, won't we? I grew up in the '80s. And while our sense of fashion might have been questionable. There was one product…that has stood the stest of time. In fact, it is the top-selling product in its market even today. Any ideas what it might be? Enter, the Rubik's Cube.

The creator of the Rubik's cube is Ernő Rubik. He wasn't a toy manufacturer, but a Hungarian Architect. He created the cube in 1974 as a 3D Model of Geometry. It wasn't designed as a toy and Ernő wasn't a brilliant puzzle creator. In fact, it took Ernő 4 months to find a solution to his own puzzle.

And when he decided to try to put it on the market to sell, the toy manufacturing companies turned him down at first, saying that Rubik's cube was too hard for the public to solve. It took him 3 years to bring it into the toy market. And now here we are, more than 45 years later, and the Rubik's Cube is still the TOP Selling TOY of all time.

Have you ever solved a Rubik's Cube? Did you know that there are over 43 quintillion possible solutions to the Rubik's Cube? What does that even mean? How do we even understand how big that is?

If you started at the beginning of time, and took a Rubik's cube and turned it every second. You would still be creating patterns that have never been created before. So if you have ever played with a Rubik's cube you should be congratulated. Even if you have never solved the puzzle...but statistically speaking, you have now been a part of a unique client experience that no one else on the entire planet has experienced. Every turn you make with this toy, means that you have just screwed it up in a way that no other person has done before you in the history of the Rubik's Cube.

Let's go back…to our buddy Ernő. He learned another important entrepreneurial lesson. He said his biggest takeaway was…that the "public wanted something different than the toy trade manufacturers could have even imagined at the time'. In other words, put your clients first. Listen to what THEY want…they will help you make some of the most important decisions about your business.

▶ Expecting the WOWs!

You should get really good at WOW!s. Take this is your opportunity to create amazing responses from your clients, customers, tribe, or community. So you may be asking what exactly is a WOW? WOW!s are quite simply the words your clients say when you surprise or delight them.

"WOW!, that's amazing!"
"WOW!, you didn't have to do that!"
"WOW!, you remembered my birthday!"
"WOW!, who does that?"

Once you recognize and start hearing these affirmations from your clients, you will wonder how you have lived without them all of these years.

So, what if, instead of worrying about the competition…

WE FOCUS ON DELIVERING AN AMAZING AND UNIQUE CLIENT EXPERIENCE?

WOW!Factor Experiences can be created using custom physical products as long as they focus on the Client-centric Connection. It's not about SWAG... these are powerful touch-points that are both Meaningful & Memorable strategic connections with your clients.

Here are some great examples of gifts that could be a WOW!Factor Experiences and special for your clients:

- PLANTS/FLOWERS
- REUSABLE BAGS
- HOME OFFICE ACCESSORIES
- DRINK-WARE
- EDIBLE GIFTS
- WELCOME GIFTS
- GIFT SETS
- KEY CHAINS/CHARMS/PINS
- OFFICE SUPPLIES
- ZEN/PEACE GIFTS

- TEAM GEAR & APPAREL
- BOOKS/BEST SELLERS
- TECH ACCESSORIES
- GIFT CARDS
- PLANNERS
- JOURNALS

What are your big WOW!Factor Experience plans? Take a moment to plan out your ideas that will make your clients go "WOW!".

____

____

____

▶ Get to know the team!

Clearly, you set your new clients up for success by getting them up-to-speed and connected with your team or other members immediately. The idea of client retention and amazing experiences can be supported by your whole team, there is no need for you to do it alone.

A handful of essentials:

- Ensure the new client is immersed from day one by outlining what your program culture looks and feels like. Have other members of your team, and even other members fill them in with more specific details, preferably in person, on zoom or through video.

- Make sure they have all information and materials needed to understand how to interact with you and your team and what is expected within community environments, including social media groups, and live events (send the information via email when possible, even a PDF outline might be beneficial).

- Be sure that someone always welcomes them personally. This can be in person, or a phone call, or coffee chat zoom call. It is critical for your clients to feel connected with from the beginning.

- Provide workbooks, journals, training manuals, and materials (including any passwords or login information needed for your client).

- Make connection fun and engaging for everyone.

▶ Video is my friend.

Where on earth would we be without the ability to connect virtually and on a global scale? Video conferencing apps, like Zoom allow us the face time we all need to feel a part of something bigger than ourselves. Seeing smiling, happy faces right off the bat sets the stage for your clients to have a positive and memorable first experience with you, your team, and your community.

Encourage your team to individually introduce themselves via a quick video chat using an app product like Bonjoro. You can also use Facebook Messenger to send quick messages to the new client. Connecting in a one-on-one space gives the new client dedicated time to get to know everyone professionally and personally.

▶ Alone no more!

Many people in this world are working remotely. Make sure to keep everyone connected by holding a virtual meeting at least once or twice a month. This will be a great way to build a connection touch-point with you, your team, and your clients. This will help everyone feel connected and a part of the big picture of your program or culture.

Or you can dedicate Friday afternoons at 5 p.m. to a virtual happy hour? You could send out a colorful beverage tumbler or coffee mug with a fun message and toast to the best clients, team, or membership ever. Connecting as a community has helped many online and live programs to grow bigger than anyone could have imagined. Clients come for the content and stay for the community. This statement has helped many entrepreneurs to connect with their clients in creative and new innovative ways, and make everyone feel less alone.

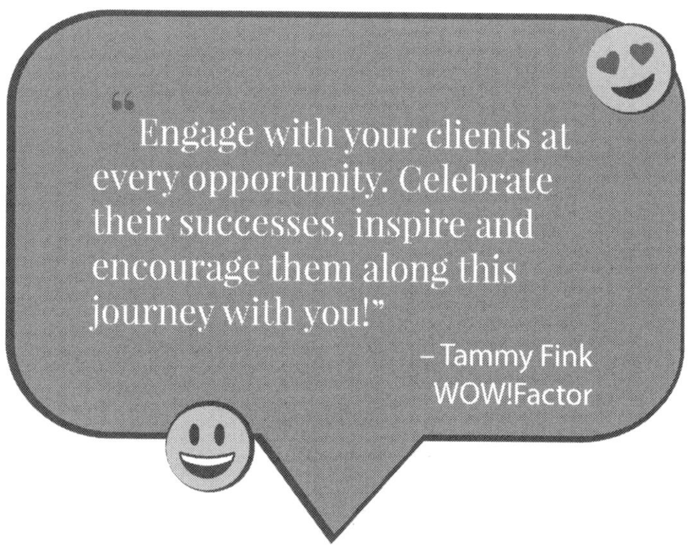

▶ Take it easy.

Overwhelm is a real thing. I have been in memberships where the information is so complete and daunting I don't even dare to get started. Giving small touch-points at the beginning of the relationship helps to encourage success with two or three initial tasks,which can be easily completed during the first week. This will introduce clients into your program at a reasonable and attainable level.

During week two, remind them that you really care with a tangible boost. It doesn't have to break the bank; even small forms of gratitude make a lasting impression. During the beginning of the relationship it is important to remind them that they are making progress, and there is more to come during their journey with you.

▶ Check in (again and again).

This one ranks way up there on the importance list—offer consistent support, communication, and check-ins. Remember: a client that feels supported is more likely to stick with you throughout the entire program.

Touch base with your client a couple times a week until you know they're completely settled in. Then reward and show appreciation as they continue to grow in their role. Milestones that are built into your process will not only help encourage your clients, but also let them know where they are in the client journey.

▶ Feedback along the way!

Be sure to get feedback from your clients. How was their on-boarding experience? Did they receive the welcome they expected, or is there room for improvement? Don't shy away from ways to improve. Strengthening your on-boarding process will only make for a more thriving business with loyal, vested clients.

:: CHAPTER FIVE ::

CLIENT RETENTION { PHASE FOUR }

There is a voice screaming in your head, "we must have more numbers." But what if there is such a rush to bring in more members, that you are totally overlooking your existing clients? We can be so caught up in the math, that we forget the humans that are already engaging with us. Even in the online space, it costs more to acquire new clients than it does to maintain existing ones. Now, think about that for just a minute...what if you focused more on client retention, and did it before they were even your client?

So much focus is put into getting new clients, that existing clients can suddenly feel not appreciated. And this can be a costly mistake. You can be losing thousands of dollars a year by not doing anything to decrease the churn and burn in your tribe. As early as 1990, the Harvard Business Review revealed that the high cost of acquiring a client could be overcome in the retention of that same client, at a reduced rate over time. Now, what does that mean to you? Overall, nurturing your connection with your clients is so much more valuable than obsessing over finding new clients. Perhaps offering a referral or affiliate program is a more cost effective way to ensure repeat business. An appreciated client will stay engaged with you, and will sing your company's praises to their peers and friends.

In 2017, I traveled to Austin, Texas to attend a three day business conference hosted by Josh & Jill Stanton. One of the keynote speakers during the event was Heather Gray, a mindset coach. Her speech was entitled 'Staying In Your Own Lane." While her speech was memorable on it's own merit, we all must admit that we are on information overload at the time of the event. However, she did something before her speech that was more powerful than perhaps she could have possibly hoped for. In fact, I think it was one of the most brilliant pieces of marketing that I have seen in quite some time.

Before she began, she passed out a large box for each table, and in the boxes were simple Hot Wheel's cars. It should be noted they were “unbranded”, meaning her logo was nowhere to be found on the cars at all. We all picked through the packages like it was Christmas morning. These $2-$3 toys made such an impact. Here is why I think they were so brilliant:

1. It was ‘Meaningful’ to the event, the cars were themed perfectly for her speech: “Stay In Your Own Lane”.

2. It was ‘Memorable” to the event.

3. It was small enough to take home in our carry-on luggage, for those of us traveling.

4. It was interactive and personal - because we were allowed to choose.

Even today, I still have mine on my desk, and I tell this story over and over and share it with people all over the world. I know where I was when I got it, the story behind it, who was speaking, and the title of her speech. What would it be worth to you to have people still talking about you three years later???

▶ The personal touch.

There are so many purpose driven entrepreneurs in the online space. Oftentimes they don't even consider offering a tangible item as an on-boarding gift, or a small token to inspire or motivate their new client. Without these personal touches, clients can feel a bit unappreciated during the warm welcome phase of the relationship. This is a completely missed opportunity to give your client warm fuzzies, and the opportunity for them to share the experience with others.

I love the idea of a hand-written sentiment. Cards are a simple way to connect with your clients. If you go this route, I encourage you to send something that is creative, unique, fun, personal, and in alignment with your brand. Make sure that it is something that will be well received and heartfelt by your client. Sending a hand-written note can even be something that you have your online community manager, or virtual assistant do for you to welcome your clients to your program. However, consider your clients first and what you want them to experience as a result of your note.

Last year, I worked with a very experienced business trainer, whose job it was to train other coaches for a particular high profile program. She had done this work for years, and had impacted hundreds of people's lives. Many people were so grateful, they would send her hand-written notes. In fact she had received hundreds of thank-you notes and cards, she had to create several large memento boxes to store them. She read and cherished every one of them I am sure. However, while notes and cards are officially a touch point, if they don't connect with your client, it can still be seen as 'Oh, isn't that nice'. It doesn't get the "WOW!" response that you were hoping for. It's the WOW! that lets you know that the connection lands and touches your client's heart.

WOW!

GREAT IDEA: Photo-cards or cute/ funny postcards usually make it to the bulletin board, or desktop status. They can be the ultimate in the hand-written note category. Avoid the generic 'Thank-You' discount store card variety.

▶ Engaging my clients.

Oftentimes, clients don't want to sit quietly consuming your content. They want to engage with other super fans, or be a part of a larger community. You can promote live events, or encourage participation within your community. Often your clients want to be a part of something larger than themselves, and they want to be a part of your story. So it is crucial for you to share that story within your tribe. If you have a 'give back' program, clients want to know how you give back to others and why. They want to be able to take part in giving back as well. Look at Tom's Shoes as an amazing example of a company and product that gives back to a community. Giving back is what they have become known for, and it's how they have differentiated themselves from any competitor in the market.

You need to establish a value for engagement and show how it impacts your tribe and community. There are networking opportunities above and beyond the traditional 'just doing business'. Seeking out and offering joint venture or co-op opportunities allows you to support other businesses within or adjacent to your niche. This way everyone wins.

Last year, I was thrilled to be able to ask Kate Erikson how she and her hubby, John Lee Dumas (of Entrepreneurs On Fire podcast fame) show gratitude to their people. This is what she shared with me:

"We've tried many different ways of showing gratitude to the members of our online communities, and really all of them have been successful in their own way. In the very beginning, it was with personal welcome calls, which we still do to this day with our Podcasters' Paradise membership that's over 3,200 members and counting! We also send out a personal video message via **Bonjoro** *to every one of our new members.*

For a while we tried sending out coffee mugs with our community logo on them, and these were also a big hit. People love receiving stuff in the mail, especially after making a big investment. We found that it really solidified trust and was a strong foundation for a continued relationship.

We also sent out a postcard and brownies via **SendOut Cards** *for a significant period of time, and we had members posting pictures in our private Facebook group every single day. Even if people didn't eat the brownies, they were still very touched by the thought. Again, we feel the act of receiving something physical and tangible goes a really long way, especially in today's online world where everything is digital. So even if it's something super small, like taking the time to give a new member a phone call to welcome them voice-to-voice, or sending out a postcard, it can make a big difference."*

- Kate & John Lee Dumas

So, when it comes to creating a WOW!Factor Experience moment, it's the little things that you do (and doing them consistently) that make a big difference. And you don't have to have a huge budget to make a huge impact. Doing small things very well can also make a huge impact. If you make it all about your client, they will throw hand-hearts your way every time.

▶ Make it fun.

Above and beyond training or coaching, customer recognition and rewards are two of the most recognized methods of motivation in today's learning strategies. However, it can be a challenge to deliver content in a way that makes it fun and engaging.

Gamification teaches us that the more engaged a client is, the longer they will stay in your program or membership. If you can show them that they are succeeding by implementing your strategies, you will succeed in higher client retention and program completion rates.

As promised in chapter two, here is a great example of gamification in a brick and mortar setting: I was fortunate to travel to Waco, Texas in 2020. So, of course I visited Magnolia, the shopping and dining premiere destination hot-spot of Chip and JoAnna Gaines originally of HGTV fame. I was thrilled to see that as part of their unique client experience, they offered a map booklet that gave information about their stores. And it contained a 'gamification' component that included collecting ink stamps from their 8 shops, including two shops that were not a part of their "Magnolia" block in the downtown area. Once you toured each shop you could ask for an ink stamp to be added to your booklet. Then upon completion you would get an exclusive "Magnolia" pin. It was a delightful way to encourage us to engage with the entire experience.

Look at these top gamification opportunities:

- Online Challenges
- Quiz/Assessment/Poll
- Learning Path Games
- Team Building Exercises
- Program Leader-boards
- Social Media Leader-boards

WOW!Factor

:: CHAPTER SIX ::

ADVOCACY { PHASE FIVE }

Word-of-mouth advertising can go a long way in this socially driven online business environment. We are so plugged-in it is almost expected for our clients to be able to 'check us out' before doing business with us. So is it any wonder that having several 5 star reviews would not only shine a spotlight on your business, but highlight your clients' success? Think of the impact this would have on your business. Testimonials provide social proof, which lets your potential clients know they can trust you. This also affirms their purchases.

Most of us understand the importance of testimonials as we have seen them in many advertisements of products we have purchased ourselves. It used to be that we could expect to see testimonials in marketing materials, sales copy, ads, and even conversations with our friends and neighbors. Living in a tourist town myself, I can't tell you the number of restaurants, hotels, and family entertainment venues I have personally recommended over the years. However, some people are just outright uncomfortable asking for, or don't know how to get great testimonials. And if and when they get them, they don't know what to do with them.

Several years ago, my husband and I were eating at a new

restaurant that we found on a little vacation trip to Eureka Springs, Arkansas. It was a cute little BBQ restaurant located in the downtown area. After we had ordered, the owner was making the rounds through the several tables of diners. She was personally checking in on each diner, which was a lovely touch to the experience. She stopped and was chatting to someone near us, and I overheard her say, "My son says that we need to be online, but I don't even own a computer. And I really just don't even see the point, so I'm not going to do the online thing." WOW. Even in this day and age, I wouldn't have believed that. But I was a witness first hand to this restaurant owner being so oblivious to the online space. But it happens. I'm not saying that you have to be tied to every part of social media, or have a huge online presence to have a successful business. However, you can't deny it or overlook that the online space exists.

Just because you may not BE 'online', doesn't mean that you aren't ALREADY 'online'. Especially when you're in a service driven business such as restaurants, among many others. If you have a physical location, you are at the very least on Google. And if you are on Google, there will be Google reviews about your establishment. Good and bad, people will be talking about you online. And you should at least know what they are saying, and how to address it. After all, it is 'FREE' advertising. And in the spirit of full disclosure, we found that little BBQ place by Googling "restaurants". There were a couple of awesome reviews for that little BBQ joint. However, it should be noted that the next year we went back to Eureka Springs, that little restaurant wasn't there. It made me wonder if it had anything to do with the owner 'not seeing the point' of nurturing an online presence.

People love to talk about their experiences, both good and bad. So doesn't it make sense to create an amazing client experience that bakes in the opportunity for conversations about your program, product, and touch-points? Since we are creating touch-points with our clients using the WOW!Factor Experience strategy, these are the things that we want people to be able to talk about and share with their friends. We are, in fact, giving them something to talk about.

While the BBQ restaurant had some naturally occurring testimonials in Google, most testimonials don't happen like that. And, if the CLIENT leaves a testimonial, it may not be the most helpful. Although we would like to be able to 'direct' how the testimonial platform is used, we must be more proactive than just leaving it to Google to distribute for us. So how do you ask for a testimonial that won't make you feel like you are imposing or being awkward in your request?

▶ When to ask for a testimonial?

There are some traditional times that will ensure you get amazing testimonials such as when you've solved their problem, they've achieved success, or have just expressed that they are extremely happy with you or your company. But let's do better than that, such as when you have a client for a specific period of time, or are launching a course or a funnel.

But a few years back, serial entrepreneur and business thought leader, Seth Godin wrote "Flipping The Funnel" where he simply said, "Give your fans the power to speak-up". He recommended using various online apps to give your clients the ability to leverage social media to 'talk about you'. He points out however, that 'most people don't have anything to say about you.' And therefore they aren't interested in promoting you. I think he could be right, but I also think that you can develop something that gives your clients *something to talk about*, and will encourage them to share (especially if you are giving it to them, and are encouraging them to share).

If you deliver an amazing client experience, people will talk about it. If you think that YOUR fans are amazing, then they will think so too. And if you mark their milestones with gifts and acknowledgments that are built into your funnel or client experience, you are giving them something to talk about. Now I do think Seth was right about giving your clients a platform such as social media, live videos, recorded testimonials. Amazing authenticity which delivers amazing returns on your investment. Testimonials/Referrals/Shares aren't just a 'nice to have', they are priceless.

▶ What do I need?

It was about 9pm when the Uber driver picked me up from the airport. He was on-time, and he even loaded my bags for me into his warm, and clean car. As I settled back into the seat for the ride, he began some of the usual chitchat. He asked about me and what brought me to Salt Lake City? I told him about the retreat where I would be speaking the next day.

I shared with him that I was a bit disappointed arriving at night, because I couldn't see any of the sights. That's when he did something that just delighted me. He began describing some of the highlights of our drive as we passed them, and at night most were lit up so that we could see them from a distance. It was an amazing ride, and maybe my best Uber experience to date.

When we arrived at our destination, I tipped him, which he probably expected. But then I did something that threw him off of his game...I asked him, "How can I help make a difference in your business?"

I could tell by his delayed response that no one had ever asked him that before. He was stunned that he didn't have to even ask me, of course I was willing to give him an amazing testimonial. But I had just had an amazing customer experience, and that could have been more valuable to his business if only he had known what to ask me for. A video testimonial? A Google review? An email to the Uber Corporation? I basically gave him a blank 'referral' check, and he didn't know how to cash it in.

Don't miss the opportunity to have someone sing your praises. But more importantly, know WHAT would be very helpful to you to attract more of the best type of client for you.

For a review or a testimonial to inspire others, it needs to say much more than 'you did a great job'! Describing why a client chose to work with your, or how your results made a difference to them may be a great place to start. Or perhaps sharing a video of a welcome box opening, or showing your product/event photos would even be better. If you aren't thinking of 'what YOU need', how can you encourage your clients to give you the best possible review or testimonial?

▶ How to use testimonials/reviews?

You can use testimonials, referrals, videos, and genuinely nice things that would be beneficial to potential clients. I recommend my clients always keep screenshots of online comments. Since these are posted in public, they can be used on your website, or posted on social media.

I also encourage box openings (whenever possible) to my clients. People want to share amazing experiences, and show what goodies they received. Do you remember as a child when your birthday or a special gift receiving opportunity came around? One of the first things we would do was call our best friends and share what we received. It was almost as much fun sharing as it was receiving the gift. People want to share the love. And when they see other people posting in your groups or communities, they want to be able to say that they have something worthy of sharing too.

Testimonials done correctly can build trust...and

community. They are more authentic than a company's statement about their own products or services. Showing before and after images or videos can clearly show the results to your future clients. Testimonials help your future customers see what your company can offer them through a marketing tactic that seems very similar to word of mouth.

▶ How do I ask ?

Once you know that a client has had an amazing experience, that is definitely the time to hit them up for a testimonial or review. Most people will gladly share their story, if you would just ask. But how do you ask?

I had a client who owned a resort, and I remember asking him once, why he didn't post a "please review us on **Trip Advisor**" sign. He gave me a lesson on the 'general public', "Some people are just looking to give bad reviews, it's like you just can't please them. They are entitled to their opinions, however you may not want to advertise to them specifically. There will always be 'online trolls' and people who just want to give bad opinions." So what do you do?

One suggestion is to create business cards that specifically give instructions on where and how to post reviews that are beneficial to you. **Trip Advisor** calls them 'custom reminder cards'. These remind your happy clients to share their amazing experience online where you need them to.

On-boarding or off-boarding surveys are a great way to test the waters for a review. Provide them with a few sample questions in an email to help them to remember their experience. This will help them to re-discover the magic. It's also an excellent touch-point in their client journey, as well as an opportunity for another WOW!Factor Experience moment. If your questions can encourage your client to open up and provide honest feedback, the testimonial will be more impactful for potential new clients. Here are some sample question ideas:

- Why did you select me for your project?

- What made you believe that I was the best for achieving (your desired result)?

- How did you benefit from working with me?

- What are the two most significant improvements that have resulted from your work with me?

- What exactly did I do to contribute to the outcome you wanted?

- What were the results of working with me?

- Describe why you feel that working with me was successful.

- What type of businesses would most benefit from working with me?

- If a potential client was on the fence about whether to work with me or not, what would you say to them?

Email is one of the easiest and convenient ways to ask for a testimonial. When you email your clients, your requests should be appropriately warm and professional so your client is reminded of why it was amazing to work with you. If you are unsure of how to get started, here are some great examples. Please change these to fit your specific needs.

Email to a client asking for a testimonial:

Dear {Client},

Working with clients like you is why I started my business in the first place. I would like to ask you to provide a testimonial that is sure to help inform potential clients why it was good to work with me and how they can benefit from such an experience themselves.

To help you get started, I've included a few questions, but please feel free to write whatever you like.

{Include two or three questions, using the Sample Question Ideas List as a guide.}

I value your business and look forward to working with you again in the future. Please let me know if there is anything further I can do for you.

Thank you in advance for your time and support,

{Your name}

Email to a client asking if you may quote them for a testimonial, this is a great way to share screenshots of comments on social media, as well.

Dear {Client},

Thank you for taking the time to express your kind comments to me. Your praise brightened my day, and clients like you make everything I do worthwhile.

I would like to share your thoughts and comments with potential clients. Your words will help them to understand how they can benefit from working with me. It would mean a lot to me to have your permission to do so.

Thank you again for your business, and please let me know if there's anything further I can do for you.

Thank you in advance for your time and support,

{Your name}

Alternatively, if an existing or previous client says something about your product or service that you think would benefit other potential clients, then simply ask them if you can use their statement. Most generally they will say 'yes'. Write it up and email it back to them, asking for per permission to use it.

▶ Don't just take my word for it!

Testimonials can also be used in conjunction with your best success stories. Take a moment and note some of the best outcomes and hero stories that you have been able to achieve for your clients, include your clients names and reach out to them asking for amazing testimonials.

GREAT IDEA: This is a great time to 'reconnect' with previous clients as well. And you will be reminding them of their amazing experience that they had with you previously.

▶ Spread the gratitude around.

Whenever a client provides a testimonial, don't forget to send them a kind thank-you note. A personal handwritten note is best for this situation, and a thank-you gift may even be a good idea in some circumstances. The goal is to make your clients feel that they've done a good thing, while also keeping your business in their minds so that they'll provide referrals and work with you again in the future.

Who do you know, who would give you a raving testimonial? Who have you helped, that you would love to help again? Those testimonials are most valuable, because it helps you to 'attract' more of those same type clients in the future.

Make a list of those people who you want to ask for testimonials, reviews, or recommendations:

Tammy Fink

:: CHAPTER SEVEN ::

NEXT LEVEL: MOMENTS THAT MATTER

This final chapter is probably the most important chapter in the entire WOW!Factor Experience book. This is where you begin thinking about your action plan for the WOW!Factor Experience in your business starting right now. Creating intentional WOW!s for your client's journey will ensure that you create a culture that is expandable and sustainable. How you interact with and love on your clients will determine how you and your program are remembered and shared with from this point forward. Once you SEE your own WOW!Factor Experience opportunities, you can't just unsee it. Things will never be the same for you and your clients.

Creating WOW!s will surpass all of your clients' expectations, and your WOW!Factor Experience will become one of your best greatest assets. Investing back into your clients ensure that you an amazing return on that investment. It will encourage more referrals, higher client retention, and loyal clients. Building these relationships will require generosity and hospitality on your part, but it will come back to you many times over.

Creating and giving WOW!s to others is an amazing way to do business, and to live your life. Celebrating life with those around you helps you to create a unique experiences and build a stronger relationships. So, I'm going to challenge you over the next 7 days to take a look at your client journey. And map out your opportunities to create WOW!s before, during, and after your program, membership, or course.

Start looking at how you can make a difference in your client's lives. Look at client engagement opportunities and how you can make them more Meaningful & Memorable. What does it look like to truly welcome your clients into your program or membership? Do they have everything they need to get started off on the right foot?

Can you invest time in your clients lives? Perhaps through events, retreats, or online communities? More and more time is spent online these days, so what about creating virtual 'coffee-chats' for you and your clients? Time is a precious commodity, but time spent with clients is always an investment worth making.

Can you create products or tools that will help your clients reach their goals and be held accountable to your program at the same time? How can you use training materials to create a culture within your business?

Celebrating your clients wins helps you to show how important your clients are to the whole process. Create celebratory moments before there is something to celebrate. This will definitely be a WOW! moment for you and your clients.

As you create the recipe for your client's experiences. Remember it is moments that will help you to differentiate yourself from your competition on every level. These experiences are meant to be heartfelt, and more meaningful and memorable than anything your client has experienced before working with you or your product.

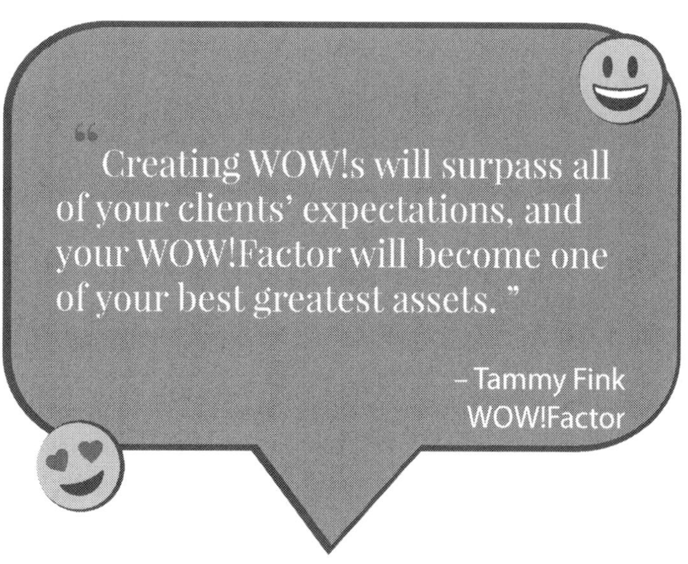

This is what the WOW!Factor is all about. Let's create amazing customer experiences that will celebrate, motivate, and inspire your clients. Hopefully these examples of the three main types of moments will inspire you. List some of those moments that would truly matter to your clients:

▶ What are my celebration milestones?

Letting your client's know that you are in the journey with them is so important. They need both encouragement along the path and acknowledgment of their successes. Creating celebrations of milestones for your clients is one way of ensuring that your clients feel seen as an important part of their journey. It's more about them, than it is about you.

1. Welcome / Onboarding
2. Halfway Point Celebration
3. Encouragement Keep Going
4. Finish Line Accomplishment
5. Stuck Points
6. ______________________________
7. ______________________________
8. ______________________________

▶ How about heartfelt moments?

Acknowledging personal moments within your client's lives matter. These heartfelt moments will help build stronger relationships. Clients want to do business with people they know, like, and trust. How can you make these moments remembered within your client's journey?

1. Birthdays

2. Community

3. Family

4. Social Media

5. Just Because

6. ______________________________

7. ______________________________

8. ______________________________

▶ Motivation and relationship building

Building strong relationships takes your client's journey to a whole new level. Some of the best times working with your clients should be easy, fun, and give extreme value. These types of experiences will not only solidify the relationships between you and your clients but also encourages bonding within the group or team. Creating a VIP retreat that allows for your clients to connect with each other and your team, this allows shared experiences that will be talked about for years to come. How can you create these types of relationship building touch-points within your business?

1. Gamification

2. Retreat

3. Challenges

4. Team Building

5. VIP Opportunities

6. ____

7. ____

8. ____

Creating your WOW!Factor Client Experience journey will not only help you to increase client retention, but it will help you stand out from the crowd. You will build devoted customers out of raving fans. Focusing on the wants, needs, and desires of your clients first will make for Meaningful & Memorable moments for them and for you - this is the Client-centric Connection framework that you will build your WOW!Factor Client Experience upon. Now go make some WOW!s for your clients today.

____

____

____

____

____

Where do you start to create your WOW!Factor Client Experience?

Why not start at HELLO?

Welcome Boxes are the Simple, Insanely Powerful Tactic that Leading Entrepreneurs, Influencers, and Coaches are Using to Build Stronger Relationship and Stand Out in the Marketplace

Join the Welcome Box Challenge and Discover the Step-by-Step Process to Creating Welcome Boxes that will Blow Your Clients Minds

And that's why the TOP ENTREPRENEURS across ALL industries are using Welcome Boxes as both a lead generation tactic and a customer loyalty strategy...

It's because they're one of the EASIEST WAYS to build connection and minimize turnover with your clients, customers, members, and students.

Period.

Welcome Boxes have proven time and time again to either surprise and delight clients or set up your students for success.

And it's an extremely powerful way to elevate the quality of both your products and services in the marketplace.

www.WelcomeBoxChallenge.com

Manufactured by Amazon.ca
Bolton, ON